I Don't Want To Live For Ever!

by Jillian Powell

GW00870463

Back Forward Stop Refresh Home Favorites History Search

Contents

Introduction

I don't want to
live for ever
... do you?

" Living for ever sounds great, doesn't it? But would it really be a good thing for us and for the world we live in? "

In stories

There are lots of myths and legends about living for ever. In some legends, it is seen as a punishment. For example, *The Wandering Jew* is a story about a man who is made to live for ever as a punishment.

In science

Some scientists think they might find a way to slow down or stop our body cells from ageing. Would this be a good thing?

secret anti-ageing formula

Section 2:
Life without death?

"All living things age and die. A butterfly lives just a few days; a tree can live to be hundreds of years old. But every living thing that you see around you will die in time: trees and other plants, mammals, birds and insects. As living things grow old and die, the young grow up to take their place. Plants and trees produce seeds; animals and people have babies."

How long do they live?

Years

Worm	Mouse	Cat	Human	Parrot	Tortoise
25 days	2 years	14 years	78 years	100 years	110 years

- Bristle-cone pines can live for thousands of years. The oldest living tree is in the White Mountains, California, USA. It is called 'Methuselah' and is said to be 4700 years old.

  The tree looks dead, but it still grows new leaves. ◄

- In the Antarctic, there are plants called lichens which can live for millions of years. They are among the world's oldest living things.

> There wouldn't be enough room for everyone!

"Now imagine if nothing ever died. What would happen? More young would be born but the old would go on living. In time, the planet would be overrun by insects, birds, animals and people. In time, there would not be enough food or water or space on the planet to keep all the living things alive."

Information

- The world has only a certain amount of water. If there are more people they will need more water. There is already a third less water for each person in the world than there was thirty years ago.

- No one knows for sure how many people can live on our planet. Some people say there are already too many.

- There are over six billion people on the planet now and 800 million people each year do not get enough food to eat.

Number of people on planet now ◄

► Number of people who don't get enough food already

Section 3:

Living a long life

" Imagine if you knew you had another 200 years to live. You would have time to have several different careers, hundreds of holidays and lots of friends. That sounds great, doesn't it? But think about it. If you really had all the time in the world, it might get boring. You would have lived so long, you might start to feel tired – like at the end of a day, when you have had enough and just want to go to sleep. "

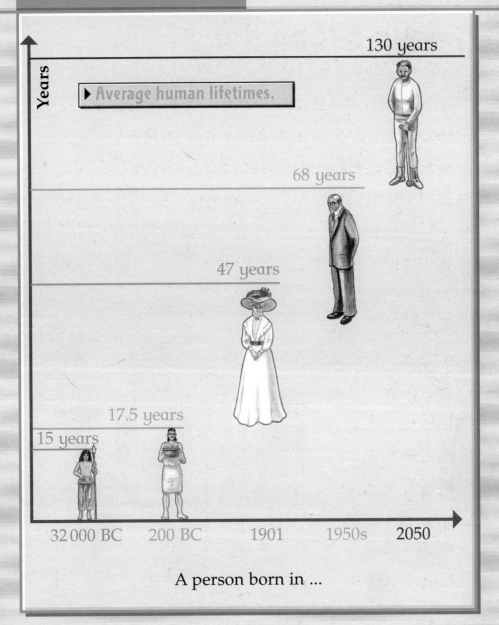

Years

130 years

▶ Average human lifetimes.

68 years

47 years

17.5 years

15 years

32 000 BC   200 BC   1901   1950s   2050

A person born in ...

Some people pack a lot into a short life.

But if we had endless time, we might not make the most of life. For example, we all enjoy a holiday, but if our holidays went on and on, they wouldn't be so special. Perhaps science can help us to live longer lives, but it can't help us shape our lives or make them happier. **"**

▶ Some people would just get bored if they could live for ever.

Some people who achieved a lot in a short life

- The composer Wolfgang Amadeus Mozart died aged thirty-five in 1791.

- The poet John Keats died aged twenty-six in 1821.

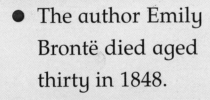

- The author Emily Brontë died aged thirty in 1848.

- The soldier Joan of Arc was burned at the stake in 1431 aged nineteen.

Section 4:

Too many changes!

" Ageing and dying are part of life. Trying to fight them goes against nature. Imagine if you were still alive at the end of the next century. You would have lived through so many changes! The music you listen to, the clothes you wear, the house you live in, all the things that are familiar to you now would have changed over and over again. Think how different it would be for people born 200 years ago, who were still living today. They would have lived though hundreds of different fashion trends. "

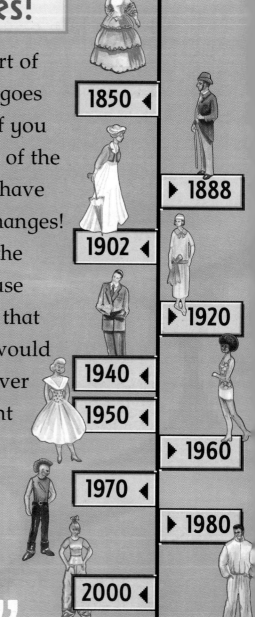

1810

1850 ◄

► 1888

1902 ◄

► 1920

1940 ◄

1950 ◄

► 1960

1970 ◄

► 1980

2000 ◄

2010

Information

> " For thousands of years, people have tried to use science to find a way for people to live for ever. Some people pay to have their bodies or heads frozen in liquid nitrogen when they die. This is called **cryogenics**. They believe that one day scientists will find a way to bring them back to life. "

▶ Some people want to be frozen so they can see the future. But how will they fit in in 200 years time?

cryogenics: the study of what happens to things at very low temperatures.

you could live for 300 hundred years, for example, your life would not follow the pattern that human lives have followed for centuries. Would this be exciting or scary? The traditional guidelines on when to have a family, when to have a career, when to retire would not apply any more. Would you start to have a family after fifty years, or two hundred years? **"**

Baby   Start   Start your   Have a   Retire

school   career   family

What makes us age?

Our bodies are made up of millions of different cells. There are over two thousand cells in your little fingernail alone. From the time we are born, our cells divide and renew themselves, but as we get older, this process slows down. Scientists know that we age when our body cells are no longer able to divide and renew themselves. They think that ageing is caused by chemicals from inside and outside the body which damage our body cells. They call these chemicals "free radicals".

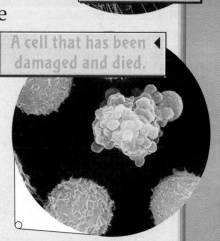

▶ Cells dividing.

A cell that has been ◀ damaged and died.

Section 5:

Will science give us the answer?

▶ Our parents, grandparents and great grandparents are much older than us.

"Some scientists think they may soon be able to find and replace the **genes** that cause ageing. This could change human lives for ever. If you could stay young for ever, your life would be very different from the lives of everyone who has gone before you."

gene: a unit in our bodies that passes from parent to child and carries our characteristics

Turning back the age clock

Every cell in a living thing contains DNA. DNA stores all the information that the cell needs when it divides to make new cells. Scientists have found that each time a cell divides some of the strands of DNA get shorter. They go on getting shorter all the time, until they are so short they tell the body cell to stop dividing. Then the body dies. But scientists have now found a way to make these strands

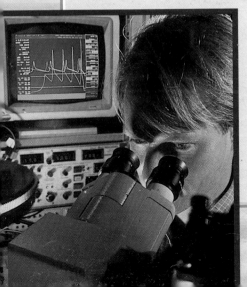

longer. They think that they may be able to use this to slow down or stop body cells from ageing and dying.

DNA

Section 6:

More people, more problems

"By helping us all to live longer, science will create new problems for us. If people go on living longer and longer, there will be more and more mouths to feed. Already millions of people in poorer parts of the world die from hunger, so how can we feed more? How can we provide enough water for everyone when there are already water shortages in some parts of the world?"

Information

- The population is growing because more babies are being born, and more people are living longer.

- In 1999, world population reached six billion.

- By 2050, world population is expected to be eleven billion. Two thirds of the world's population could then face water shortage.

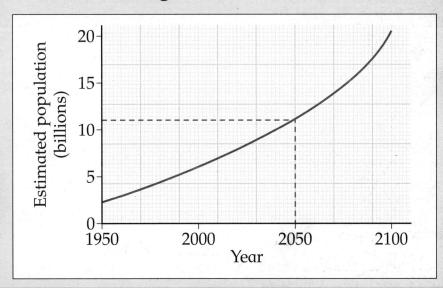

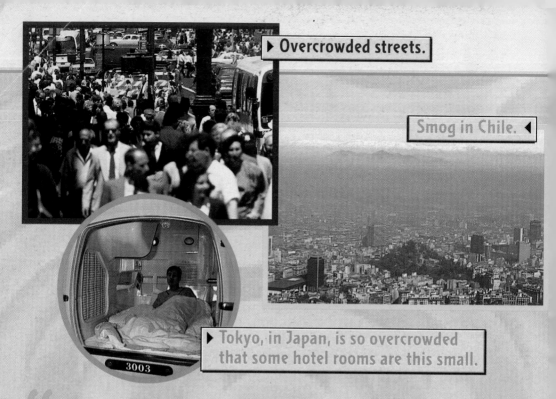

▶ **Overcrowded streets.**

Smog in Chile. ◀

▶ Tokyo, in Japan, is so overcrowded that some hotel rooms are this small.

"Where there are too many people, there are many problems. Cities become more crowded and more polluted. Diseases spread more easily. There is more crime and violence. People fight over land and **resources**. As the number of cars increases, the roads become more crowded. If there are too many people in the world, we may have to take turns for everything we do. "

resources: supplies of things we need to live

- The number of cars worldwide is expected to double to 1000 million by 2025.

  '1000 million!'

- In some countries, there are already so many cars on the roads that people have to take it in turns to drive into town. Your number plate decides which day is your turn.

"As the world gets more crowded, our lives will change. There will not be enough land or water for us to raise farm animals, so we will not be able to eat so much meat. We may have to ration fuel if there is not enough to go round. Think what this will mean. There may not be enough petrol to run our cars, or electricity to work our computers, or fridges or televisions."

Information

- It takes a hundred times more water to produce 1 kilogram of meat than it does to produce 1 kilogram of grain.

- Some experts think that fossil fuels like oil and natural gas will run out in less than a hundred years.

- Some experts think we are already consuming a third more resources than the planet can keep up with.

Section 7:

An older world

"On average, the population of the world is getting older because we are all living longer. By 2050, there will be more people over the age of sixty than there are children. If the world population goes on ageing, there will be fewer people working to make money, and more people who need support. The world will face a crisis: how can we make enough money to support all the people?"

▶ Adults will have to work even harder to support an ageing population

The world is getting older

- The number of people over the age of sixty will double by 2025.

- By 2050, there will be six times as many people over the age of eighty as there are now.

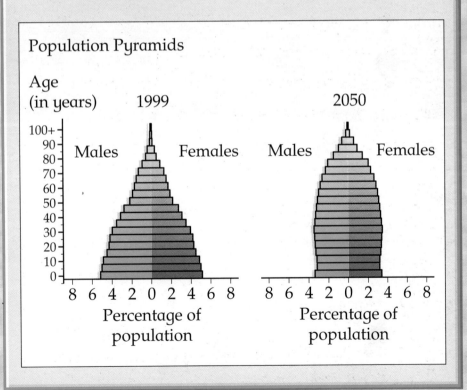

Population Pyramids

Section 8:
An ageless world?

" Some scientists say that in future we may be able to choose to stay at one age all our lives. If you could choose to remain at one age for ever, what age would you choose?

Some people look better and feel more confident in their thirties than they did in their teens and twenties.

How would you decide when to stop your own age clock? "

- Scientists are already talking about working on ways to grow new body parts. People will be able to replace worn out parts, change body parts they don't like, or design their own body.

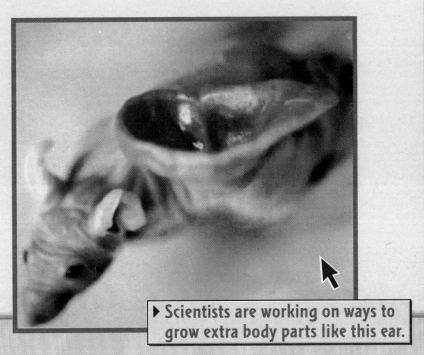

▶ Scientists are working on ways to grow extra body parts like this ear.

" What would it be like if people could choose their own age?

Imagine a world where everyone was about the same age. There would no longer be children, grown-ups, and

older people. Your parents and your grandparents might choose to stay – and look

– the same age as you and your friends are. Don't we need to have people of different ages in the world? "

Old people and young people both contribute to the world in different ways

- Older people have learned from experience: they can teach young people skills and trades.

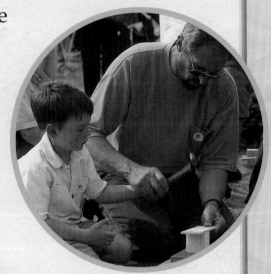

- Younger people often have more energy and new ideas.

Section 9:
Summing up

These are the arguments about why living for ever might **not** be a good thing.

● The world would get too crowded. ◀

▶ ● There would not be enough food or water for everyone.

▶ ● Pollution would increase.

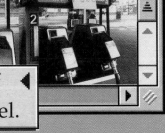

● The world would run out of natural resources such as fuel. ◀

It would be hard to give a shape to our lives.

A person would go through too many changes.

1850 ◀

2000 ◀

Life might seem too long and pointless.

The world would not have a mixture of young and old people living together.

What do you think?

Section 10:

Index